For Instance

JOHN CIARDI

For Instance

W · W · NORTON & COMPANY

NEW YORK · LONDON

FIRST EDITION

Some of these poems have appeared in *The American Scholar, Antaeus, Bits, The Blue Unicorn, The Devil's Millhopper, Impact, New Catholic World, Poetry Magazine, Review La Bouche, Saturday Review, Tamarisk, Tristram Magazine.*

The text of this book is composed in photocomposition Palatino. Display type is Typositor Windsor. Manufacturing is by the Vail-Ballou Press. Design by Marjorie J. Flock.

Library of Congress Cataloging in Publication Data
Ciardi, John, 1916–
  For Instance.
  I. Title.
PS3505.I27F6 1979   811'.5'2   79-11571

ISBN 0-393-01255-7 cloth edition
ISBN 0-393-00939-4 paperback edition

1 2 3 4 5 6 7 8 9 0

for George Garrett,
in place of a loving cup.

CONTENTS

Machine

On the Patio

Trying to Feel Something

Machine

Machine

It goes, all inside itself. It keeps touching
itself and stinks of it. The stink
moves a wheel that moves an arm that moves everything.

Or it hunches like a fetus and spins
its own umbilicus till it sparks.
Hands off, or it sizzles your hair straight!

Sometimes it turns its back, clicks,
and spits things down a chute.
It has many ways to its own kind.

Sometimes it breaks, battering itself
and must be stopped or we shall all
be saved. But it is always stopped. There is

no salvation. When it dies, we melt it
and make another that looks different
no better but does more of the same faster.

It can disguise itself as anything
but fools no one. There is always that look
of being inside itself, always that stink.

Bicentennial

This official bicentennial arts person programming
state-wide culturals for the up and coming
year-long Fourth of July, made an appointment,
and came, and I said I would (what I could),
and she said, "Are there any other New Jersey
poets we should mention?" And I said,
"Well, William Carlos Williams to start." And she:
"Has he published books?"
               And I saw hall on hall
of stone glass buildings, a million offices
with labels on glass doors. And at the first desk
in every office, nothing. And beyond, in the inner
office, nothing. And a lost wind going, and doors
all swinging bang in the wind and swinging bang.
And at the end of every corridor
a wall of buttons blinking data dead.

Worthies

Said Edward R. Murrow abroad casting
the London Blitz: "Once more the British people
have proved they are worthy of their ancestors."
And thirty-three mind-wasted years later
didn't some idiot writing for SR
quote that as an example of in-depth-of?
—Which maybe, baby. I can tell you in depth
that when the wailers began to churn where I was
I tried ancestrally—baby, didn't I try!—
to prove I was as worthy as Peking Man
to go some fathoms down and dig me later.
True, all I got from him in those family beds
I dug for religion was a fossil sneer,
but what does he know? Any ancestor
worth being worthy of would have descended
to something better. And which of our idiocies
got its bent genes from any but those worthies
Overkill's ticking to make us worthy of?

For Instance

A boy came up the street and there was a girl.
"Hello," they said in passing, then didn't pass.
They began to imagine. They imagined all night
and woke imagining what the other imagined.
Later they woke with no need to imagine.
They were together. They kept waking together.
Once they woke a daughter who got up
and went looking for something without looking back.
But they had one another. Then one of them died.
It makes no difference which. Either. The other
tried to imagine dying, and couldn't really,
but died later, maybe to find out,
though probably not. Not everything that happens
is a learning experience. Maybe nothing is.

Alec

At ninety-seven my uncle found God heavy.
"My legs," he sighed, "May I go before they do."
So small an ambition: could it be asking too much
even from a universe? It or luck

spun him the answer he wanted. Sometimes we win.
I was in Asia and missed the funeral,
all but a postcard C/O AM. EX., BANGKOK.
I bought gold leaf and rubbed a Buddha for him,

my shoes at the door, with feet left to put in them.
His name was di Simone, which is "of Simon."
He could not read, but his family legend whispered
of a turned Jew centuries back. He married

my mother's sister and passed as Alec the Barber,
though really Alessio. The gold leaf crumbles.
It makes sparks on the floor like lathe-curlings.
But some of it sticks. In time the God turns gold

and we are all one family. Back in my shoes,
I fed beggars in his name for the plains-wide days
he walked me for quail or pheasant or what comes
in or out of season. "God," he would say

"sends birds, not calendars." He was right a while,
but calendars come, too. I must have loved him,
and did not know it till I fed beggars for him
and gilded an unfinished god in its vault.

Thematic

Estrid the Conqueror raised seven red-handed
sons, all lopped in the Conquest, and he bloodlet
too pale to recruit such captains again.

It was a famous grief and long in the practice
of ethnic tragedians, though Estrid ruled
less than a six month's rage, the throne

gone to an idiot nephew whose reign ground on
through so dull a peace, three generations of poets
tick-tocked time without recording his name.

So much for the great emotions. All art knows
passion is what matters. Yet one may ask:
whose? to whom? in which of the lost kingdoms?

Two for Gertrude Kasle

The trouble with the avant garde of the Seventies is that it has
taken it fifty years to be behind the avant garde of the Twenties.

I. The Abstract Calorie

A doughnut is no sculpture.
Or anything is, and art is

theory, the assertion of theory,
the performance of the assertion.

Theoretical doughnuts (to assert)
are conceptually edible:

to the abstract gut
the abstract calorie.

A ten ton concrete doughnut
is not a ten ton concrete doughnut.

It is an assertion about doughnutry
as a condition of the human condition,

especially that of people who assert
ten ton concrete doughnuts.

II. The Title of the Last Poem Was Wrong Again

Put a dot in an infinite plain:
it is nowhere. Frame any part
of that plain and put your dot
inside the frame: you have placed it.

Now place a second dot inside:
you have drawn the invisible line
connecting your two dots. The rest
must be learned slowly, but now

it can be—*if* you are a learner
—and *if* you are not only willing
to live it as if it made a
difference, but helpless not to.

On Passion as a Literary Tradition

Asked by a reporter out of questions
to name the one thing most important to art,
Lytton Strachey, an old man with the voice
of an uncracked boy soprano, trebled, "Passion!"

It *can* treble. There's no one place on the scale
where burning starts. It can sound silly
and still be what it is. But what is it?
Housman said he had to be careful while shaving

not to think of poetry. A line
could shake him till he nicked himself.
If it cuts, it must be something. Not-much
can be enough to bleed for.

                          Foghorn Odysseus
(he *had* to be gravel throated) nocking arrows
like check marks down the guest list, did what he did
and said nothing about it. He growled instructions
to have the mess cleaned up, and took a bath.

Nikos Katzanzankis, in his version,
had a lot to say about his hair, like fire
up from the crotch to a black smoke in the armpits.
But Odysseus only grunted and reached for a towel.

Whatever passion is, it needn't tremble.
It slashes more than it nicks, can tear the guts
out of the nothing said. If you could say it,
it wouldn't be what you meant. It's a fire

that curls like hair on ape-man. It's mostly tiresome.
You need it like adrenalin when you need it
for getting up the tree ahead of the bear
who sniffs and decides you wouldn't be worth the climb.

—Or so you hope. Once then the beast is gone,
the sooner you stop pumping the stuff, the better
you'll find your bearings out of the fangy woods,
and go home to nick yourself on poetry.

Birthday

A fat sixty-year-old man woke me. "Hello,
Ugly," he said. I nodded. Ugly's easy.
"Why don't you punch yourself in the nose?" I said,
"You look like someone who would look better bloody."
"—And cantankerous," he said. "But just try it:
it's you will bleed." I shrugged. What difference
would that make? Everyone's bleeding something.

He saw me duck out the other side of the shrug.
"Where are you going?" —"Not far enough: I'll be back."
I climbed the maple that grew through our sidewalk once,
and looked at the river with Willy Crosby in it.
A man was diving. Two were in the boat:
one rowing, one working the hooks. The hooker shouted.
I was out of the tree and on the bank—where I'd been

before I remembered wrong. Willy was paler
than all the time I had taken to remember,
but I put on my Scout shirt and went to the wake.
It was better than the Senior Class Play later.
I got the part as the dead boy's best friend.
When his mother and father got tired of keening for Willy,
they turned and keened for me. "Oh, John," they wailed,

your best friend's gone! Oh, Willy, poor John's here!
Come out and play!" I could have been with Willy,
as pale as he. And when he wouldn't come out,
they sang me to him. "Oh, Willy, we bought you a suit!
Oh, Willy, we bought you a bed with new silk sheets!
Oh, Willy, we bought you a house to put the bed in!
The house is too small! Come out and play with John!"

—"Why?" said the fat ugly sixty-year-old man.
"Not that I mind dramatics, but what's the point
of hamming it up without a line to tatter?"
"Goodbye," I said. He smirked. "Well, it's a start:
at least it's a speaking part. But it's not that easy.
I won't be said goodbye to. Not by you."
"No?" I said. "Just wait a little and see

how little it costs to kiss you off, friend. Meanwhile
—hello, Ugly." He nodded. "Ugly's easy.
Easier than climbing a tree that isn't there."
"It's there," I said. "Everything's always there."
"Your lines get better," he said, "but they stay pointless."
I shrugged: "You live by points. . . ." But he stopped me.
"Don't shrug away," he said, "There's nowhere to go."

Kool Whip

That's it. The last of the heavy cream
and the old cow dead of over-grazing
astroturf. If I permitted
some ambiguity in "I love you,"
time goes toward clarities. I confess
all my ingredients to the label
and accept the freeze-dried universe.
Come. Confess with me. We never
really meant to be real. Who'd dare?
The dead beast sulks in body odor.
The stain cannot leak through this grass
to all-flowered Heaven's recycling. Come
bearing deodorants. O thumbs,
let spray the fullness of lilies. Tonight
at the sperm bank, at the planned descent
of improved angels, when one Word
is Before and After, come in witness.
As Glaucus, eating seaweed, found
a nature beyond nature; as Yeats
put by his animal to begin
the feast of artifice; come dine
on milk of mannequins who sing,
"Our peace is in His processing".

The Sorrow of Obedience

The lieutenant ordered me to ask Abdhul
    if he would sell one of the speckled puppies
    his mongrel bitch was mothering.

As I waited for Abdhul to finish cleaning his rifle
    —he is known to be testy—I reviewed the difference
    between "puppy/son of a dog" and "bitch/mother".

Obedience, as even generals must understand,
    is no substitute for idiom. I translated,
    praying to get it right once. When, however,

Abdhul first shot the lieutenant, then slit his throat,
    then lopped his sex and threw the mess to the mongrel,
    I was once more left to grieve for my imperfections.

Snickering in Solitary

(A found poem. The first four lines are exactly quoted from the
New York *Times Book Review*.)

The birdman of Alcatraz
once sold J. Edgar Hoover
a sparrow dyed yellow
and told him it was a canary.

In every life sentence
some days are better than
others; even, sometimes,
better than being free.

Scene Twelve: Take Seven

It is in its way like bumping into
an ex-wife in the lobby of the Ritz.
You do not go there often. For her
it is a habitat and she togged for it
by all of evolution. "Bill!" she says,
"how well you look!" —the grace
of all her small-talk is also from evolution:
you know how you are looking, have settled for it.
What you cannot settle is what to remember
of how much you wanted, how little
you could at last bear. —Like that.
Exactly. Everything. All the way in the taxi
and train to the other mail slot, through which
you fall and lie unread, blaming no one,
knowing you were written with nothing to say.

October 18: Boston

. . . came gift-wrapped from the liquor store. A bum
who looked like Einstein in a trash can said,
"My need is great." I dropped change in his palm
—an acknowledgement of style—and he left it there.
"Like you," he said, "I need a jug. It's cold
under the bridge, and four bits is no heat."

It was argument in order. He had asked mercy.
I had given dismissal. I shifted my bottles,
dug out my wallet, found a five. "I'm Fritz,
in case we meet again," he said, "and we may
because I live again. Thank you in reason."

—I was paying for this performance. Why should he
have all the good lines? I'm an actor, too.
"In reason," I said, "die well."

                                He had half turned.
He half turned back. "Well," he said, "is soon.
As ill is dry. You're a philosopher,
or five bucks worth of something, and will yourself
learn in time enough."

                        —And left for the bridge.
Or wherever scene-stealers go to taste their triumph.

Being Called

A breakfast reverie in Key West

The Resident Dispenser of Bromides
being included in the general call
after yesterday's train wreck,
packed his bags and went running
with pink pills for the maimed.

What can I offer, doctors, but the will
to be included when the call comes?
Perhaps to assist at triage? At least
to pronounce the dead? —As the one-armed
surgeon still advises at transplants.

He could not bring himself to retire
after his accident. As God
stayed on after His to advise Tillich
on the good it does to do good
after it no longer matters

to Heaven or concept. It is not
not caring, but only that we are
futile. Like the movie queen
who lost her looks but kept old reels
for private viewing (it still runs on TV),

we try to remember as if we still were
what we remember. There is, of course,
power in a name. Once up in lights
it never dims entirely. The old
glow back in it. Late-Lates return it

to the young, who call it "funky," meaning
"hey, wow!" (but at root, "mildewed, earthy").
—Always that next jargon for saying again,
half-lively, what turns futile.
Would it be better not to say? not

to refuse the offered no-help
of good intention? —Not that I hurt,

or only a little, of some imagined
honesty. I am in Florida,
a February rose nodding

over my toast and coffee in a soft
expensive breeze I can afford,
in a sun I buy daily, gladly,
on a patio under a lime tree.
There is a pleasantness. With luck

it is a kindly long trip down
from cramming winter to this basking
knowledge of nothing. And from Miami
on the make-do transistor, a cracked
wrong quaver that began as Mozart.

On the Patio

On the Patio

The rose at the edge of my tax structure
        sways in the breeze before twilight.
Ribbons of a scent that snares me
        whorl from it. I imagine I see them.
Like spirals flowing from Venetian glass.
        It is an air like glass I sit to.
Need it be real to be real enough?
        How real are angels?—yet Vaticans
have bedrocked on an air they stirred. As I
        have ground my hands black, even bled a little,
to turn a fantasy of a sort: the bed
        is weeded, pruned, mulched, watered.
I have paid the taxes on it. Roses
        are not for nothing. I have done
what pleased me painfully. Now I sit
        happy to look at what I look at.

When has a rose been looked at enough?
        A petal can be a shell of lemon
marked at the hinges like a pitted peach
        thumbed open warm from the tree,
but veined paler. What an intricate
        precision it takes to call a bee,
another and another intricacy veining
        to the heart of the rose—the "yellow"
as Dante knew it before hybridizers
        stained some strains red to the core
(though pinks and whites still wash to a yellow center).
        In being intricate nature is pliable.
By growing intricate enough I may yet
        come to see what I look at.
It is not easy. It is better than easy:
        it is joyously difficult. It is never
what one expected before looking. Tomorrow
        I must spray for aphids before they come,
and pay the Lawn Shop something on account.

Are accounts an offense to nature? With my hand
        I can reach six inches into the soil of that bed.

That is not nature, but makes roses. By frost time
    the tree rose must be burlaped and laid flat,
half its roots folded, the other half let loose,
    then buried again in moss and old compost,
hay, if I can find it (which I doubt),
    and then more burlap (which I have not yet paid for).
But the grafts have taken. They should bear next year
    four-colored from one stem. If that,
as I believe, is a loveliness, and not
    mere ingenuity of contrivance
(which it is, of course, but still lovely)
    it is budgeted for a grafting knife, tape, wax,
cans of Miracle-Gro, a sprayer, sprays.
    Add what the root stock cost me: a time ago
I ate for a semester on something less
    than a rose comes to. Not that price matters.
Until you haven't got it. I still have,
    and note it to pay gladly for what I buy,
wanting it more than what I spend.
    As I read catalogues for their complications.
It is not simplicity I am waiting to see
    but the rose that will not come easy
and must be painstaken beyond nature.

Suburban

Yesterday Mrs. Friar phoned. "Mr. Ciardi,
    how do you do?" she said. "I am sorry to say
this isn't exactly a social call. The fact is
    your dog has just deposited—forgive me—
a large repulsive object in my petunias."

I thought to ask, "Have you checked the rectal grooving
    for a positive I.D.?" My dog, as it happened,
was in Vermont with my son, who had gone fishing—
    if that's what one does with a girl, two cases of beer,
and a borrowed camper. I guessed I'd get no trout.

But why lose out on organic gold for a wise crack?
    "Yes, Mrs. Friar," I said, "I understand."
"Most kind of you," she said. "Not at all," I said.
    I went with a spade. She pointed, looking away.
"I always have loved dogs," she said, "but really!"

I scooped it up and bowed. "The animal of it.
    I hope this hasn't upset you, Mrs. Friar."
"Not really," she said, "but really!" I bore the turd
    across the line to my own petunias
and buried it till the glorious resurrection

when even these suburbs shall give up their dead.

Knowing Bitches

I was spading a flower bed while the old dog
inspected the lawn for memories of rabbits.
We used to have them till he hunted them out.

He walks the way I spade: it gets done
if there isn't much to do, but keeps pausing
to look back, or to look at anything.

I hadn't been listening to the bitch next door.
Her rave had become a background noise. It changed.
She had wormed under the fence and was coming mean

and meaning to be heard. I threw a clod
that spun her into circles. One of them
cut twice through my peonies. I gave a shout.

Ponti and his boys came running and shouting.
My boys came running and shouting. It would have done
for a race riot: *death to peonies!*

—Except for the old dog. He went on sniffing.
People and bitches are noisy but the earth's
to sniff and think about. When she broke through

he didn't even look up till she tried a nip.
Then, with no parts to his motion, he knocked her over
and stood astride her belly, his jaws at her throat,

not biting, then walked away stiff-legged
while she crawled after, belly to the grass,
till Ponti caught her collar and hauled her back

ravening at the leash. We waved "that's that".
I finished spading and sat on the patio.
The old dog finished sniffing and sprawled by me.

The boys found something else to shout about.
With luck and staking the peonies might come through.
The thing about bitches is knowing who *you* are.

Craft

A cherry red chrome dazzle
with white racing stripes
screams into my drive spilling
hard-rock enough to storm Heaven,
and young insolence sits there
honking for Benn, who's not in.

I put down my book
and press the crafty button
that works the black paint spray,
and press the crafty button
that jabs spikes through the drive
into all four wheels at once,

and press the crafty button
that blows his radio circuits.
Then move the crafty lever
that works the axle snips.
I am happy in my craft;
glad to learn ways to live.

Why does the blare not stop?
He does stop honking.
He slams into the house:
"Couldn't you hear me?"
"I have tried not to," I say, "is that
your radio or the fire siren?"

He beams. "Great sound, huh?"
Then: "Where's Benn?" "In earshot,"
I tell him. "Everything must be."
"Well, is he here or not?"
"He left for Boston this morning."
"Boston, huh? Well, tell him I was here."

"He knows," I say. "It's only
two hundred and fifty miles.
That's within earshot."
"Huh?" he says, wrinkling his nose.

I press my last craftiest button,
but the servo-genie

has shorted out. The trap door
does not open. There is no oil
in the kettle under the floor
and it is not boiling. He does
leave—in a four wheel drift
that smokes the turn-around—

without killing himself,
nor skidding into my arbor again.
That's as near a good as craft
could have worked it. It takes none
to know he'll work it out himself
some loud night on the Interstate.

January 1

If calendars are square holes, something
has slipped a round-peg late March morning
into this opening. A New Year's Day
smelling of wet root? I half look for crocuses,
glad not to find. We're wrong enough already.

By way of omen, we're one second late.
Astronomers ticked it onto the last minute
of the dead year. It's their accounting
for our eccentric rotation. As if one tick
could change us back to time. And yet in time—

in time enough—all seasons would drift loose
but for such finicals; as they did once
in Julian time, the vernal equinox
precessing through the centuries toward June.
We can learn to be more accurate than we have been.

Even corrected we're wrong. If that tick's true,
this day rings wrong to feeling. A New Year's Day
smelling of wet roots! Let the dog run it
as if gifts were free. I thumb a forsythia bud:
is it too soft for this side of sun shadow?

I mean to know. I get the pruning shears
and cut some stems to see if they will force.
Indoors again, I put them in a vase
and the vase on the mantel still decked out with holly,
the last dry scratch of Christmas. If this starts

let the dog shed—I may myself go bald
on gullied lawns—and leather apples shrivel
in the stubble of all season gone to random.
Just as it felt inside that astronomers' tick
added to the rung year, correcting zero.

Between

I threw a stick. The dog
ran to fetch, but dropped it
and began to dig, right there
in mid-lawn, clawing up
four half-curled baby rabbits
the size of Italian sausage,
two gulps apiece to him. Then
found the stick and fetched,
and I threw, and he fetched.

Bashing the Babies

Easter, 1968

Sometimes you have hardly been born
when a king starts having dreams about you.
His troops get drunk then—they have to—
and a baby-crop sub-generation is torn
out if its mothers screams and bashed:
orders are orders.
                    You yourself were rushed
out of the kingdom and lived to become a reader.
(I am a poet, and talk poetry. A man,
and talk chances. A son, and live as I can.
And was a soldier, killing for my leader.
And was taken by wrong parents, though their flight
is proof they could be sometimes, someways, right.)

I submit we should do or at least say
something deliberate and reasoned now
about the bashed babies. That it was they,
not we. That the feast is ours, you
its superintendent. I?—no one comes through
that infantry untouched. I am in this, too—
a father, a son, where every day
half-masted smokes wave masses, and the press
wires back body counts to the nearest guess.

It is Easter. I rise fat, rich,
hand out chocolate eggs, later drink coffee,
smoke. My dog gulps the poverty
of India heaped in an aluminum dish:
meat, egg, milk, cereal, bone meal,
cod liver oil.
                    How shall we not feel
something for the babies who could not leave town?
who were not German Shepherds? who were hit
by their eggs and burned?
                    A few, of course, make out:
some mothers are shrewd hiders, some have known
a trooper—the occupied live as they can—
and even a drunken trooper is partly, in secret, a man.

But that evades the question. Being neither drunk
nor presently commanded, having run out
and made it to luck and, possibly, dispassion—what
do we do now? After creative funk?
After picketing flags? After burning the first draft
of everyone's card? After turning right? left?

We are—I believe you—one another's question.
How do we ask ourselves? Half-masted purple
burns from crosses. A genuflection
dips dark, rises golden. The spring-wound people
of Godthank heap flowers
in stone arches. "Come walk green,"
say the bashing bells of Sunday. "This world, ours
shines for you questioner. What will you mean
by what you ask us? What shall we
mean by what we answer? What are we born to be?"

—I am a ghost, and talk vapors. An easy man
tossing a stick for a dog on an Easter lawn,
and talk my own babies, that they grew
chocolate-lucky. Your man, and talk you,
because we were together and got away
without being bashed, and would like to have
        something to say.

Any suggestions?—Well, have a good day.

Commutation

for Walker Percy

A divorced ex-nun on a commuter train
reading a book about alienated commuters
looks up and sees Newark as phenomenology
in the glazed eyes of God under their pennies.

I, too, had the dead described to me, and was promised
I need not lie among them. It was a loving
misrepresentation, like a flavored dose
meant to be good for me, that did no harm.

I have passed among them and been done no harm.
Their books about us, between us and what we are,
describe us recognizably. One can choose
to be recognized and to accept the description.

The dead are always describable. The ex-nun
has changed her mind about them. I have changed mine
a half-thought nearer being, which comes to nothing,
but leaves some choice of the possible ways we take there.

It does not promise, though promises have been made.
I, too, try reading. At Oaklawn I look up
and imagine I recognize the graves of a few
who have recognized us and have since forgotten.

From a Train Window

Someone is growing peonies
in the yard of an ugly house.
The train goes by ugly houses
all the way into Newark,
where everything stops.

Whoever is growing the peonies
should have pinched off the side buds
and staked the stems.
There are too many blossoms too small
and mostly blown flat.

Peonies come from Japan.
They are court flowers, sometimes trees.
Sun-God Emperors came silken
to meditate by them. Their odor
is called "Breath of Heaven".

All that is over now.
I think the person who grew the peonies
is dead, and that whoever lives now
in the ugly house doesn't know,
or is used to looking at Newark,
and can't see.

Censorship

Damn that celibate farm, that cracker-box house
with the bed springs screaming at every stir,
even to breathe. I swear, if one of us
half turned they'd shriek, "He's getting on top of her!"

Her father, but for the marriage certificate,
would have his .30-.30 up my ass.
Her mother, certificate or not, could hate
a hole right through the wall. It was

a banshee's way to primroses that fall
of the first year in that hate-bed wired
like a burglar alarm. If I stood her against the wall,
that would quiver and creak. When we got tired

of the dog-humped floor we sneaked out for a stroll
and tumbled it out under the apple tree
just up from the spring, but the chiggers ate us whole
in that locked conspiracy of chastity

whose belts we both wore all one grated week
while virtue buzzed a blue-fly over that bitch
of a bed hair-triggered to shriek:
"They're going at it! They're doing it right now!"—which

we damned well couldn't, welted over and on
as if we were sunburned. And every night at two
her mother would get up and go to the john,
and the plumbing would howl from Hell, "We're
        watching you!"

For Jonnel out of the Album

I changed the baby, fed it, dithered
and got dithered at, with a grin added
and arms and legs pumping,
which means "Hug me!" So I hugged
small as anything is done soft.

There was that hour once in a cone of light.

Outside the cone, the dithering universe.

I have been here, and some of it was love.

11:02 A.M. The Bird Disappeared

A humming bird darning the trumpet vine
pokes in, pokes out, pauses to look at the work.
What holds it up? Yes, wings—if this is a test
for the Civil Service and "wings" is one of the choices.
But shouldn't wings leave some blur? A hue—
as propellors darken a circle of air? This
leaves no trace. It is. And now it's gone.
And somewhere an Examiner shakes his head.

Saturday, March 6

One morning you step out, still in pajamas
to get your *Times* from the lawn where it lies folded
to the British pound, which has dropped below $2.00
for the first time since the sun stopped never
setting on it, and you pick it up—
the paper, that is—because it might mean something,
in which case someone ought to know about it
(a free and enlightened citizenry, for instance)
and there, just under it—white, purple, yellow—
are the first three crocuses half open, one
sheared off where the day hit it, and you pick it up,
and put it in water, and when your wife comes down
it's on the table. And that's what day it is.

Three A.M. and Then Five

"Do you like your life?"
said the ghost of God-shadow
one wisp of a night blowing.

"You woke me to ask that?"
I growled through the phlegm of sleep.
"What else would wake you?" it said.

I wallowed in that wind forever,
the sheets a hair shirt,
practice praying to no address.

Till my wife said, "Please lie still!"
So I went down into the wind
to where I had left the bourbon.

"No one knows me better," I told it.
"What do you think?"
"I may be too good for you," it said.

But it gentled, glowed, at last
whispered, "Go to sleep now."
I went back, the bed warm with her,

the sheets satin.
"Yes," I said to the ghost
yawningly, "Yes. Yes."

Trying to Feel
Something

Trying to Feel Something

Someone is always trying to feel something
or feeling something he'd rather not, and maybe
doesn't really—though how can one be sure?

Sylvia, John, and Anne did not entirely
invent what they felt.
                    For a few hundred cash
the shrink my lawyer made me take my son to
as a first fiction toward getting him off probation
came up with "lacunae in the super-ego"
—meaning he lost his temper.
                        So did I
listening to Judge Rocksoff, that illiterate
sac of mediocrity composing:
"This is Juvenile Court. I am Judge and Jury.
I say this evidence is incredulous. (sic)
—And you shut up!"
                    But a thousand and some later
my son was a legal adult and was learning to hide
the pot he smoked. And a million ago Sylvia
inhaled her oven. And in another million,
Anne, her exhaust. And John went off the bridge-rail
at plus-or-minus some insolvency looking
for Hart Crane maybe. None of them entirely
invented their feeling, and two of them learned to write—
which can be relevant come time to appeal
the probations imposed upon us by the illiterate,
but does seem possibly a bit fanciful
to what I have just read, over morning coffee,
of a gent in a green Ford who last night,
having driven into the South Bronx by mistake
with the thermometer at almost ninety,
happened to hit and kill a dog, and then
forgot to keep going. He stopped to say he was sorry.

To prove which, some of the boys turned over the Ford
with him inside it, and having nothing to do,
set fire to it, and having nothing to do
and the weather too hot to do it, watched a while,
then watched the firemen come, and dumped some bricks—

not many and with no malice—from the roofs,
having nothing to do, and then it was all over
and only eleven o'clock or a bit after
and too hot for sleep, and what do you do next
but sit and invent the nothing there is to feel
about what wasn't really done in the first place?

—As I sit here in Metuchen and think to invent
something to feel about something I haven't entirely
made up from nothing—except, how does one know?
Isn't the news whatever we choose to notice?
I could have turned to the daily crossword puzzle
with nothing to feel but a generalized small sadness
for the failure of definition—which takes no feeling,
or we're enured to it, which comes to the same

except that my teachers told me and I in turn
told my students that if you want entirely
to learn to write (which can be something to do)
you must first feel something
                                    except, what is there
this side of Anne's exhaust, Sylvia's oven,
John at the rail, Nixon in San Clemente,
Anne Frank and Cinderella at their chimneys,
and my coffee growing cold, which tastes blah,
though I drink it anyway for something to do?

No White Bird Sings

Can white birds sing? An ornithologist
told me once there was a white bell bird
that rang whole tones, though only as separate notes.
"Is that singing?—sound without sequence?"
I said. "No, not exactly," he granted,
"but it is white." I granted him half a case.
This morning I heard a mocking bird again
and claimed my whole case back: no white bird sings.

I know some black poets who have been waiting
for just this image. So there it is, man:
an accident, but accidents are to use.
What else is a poem made of? Well, yes, ghosts.
But ghosts are only what accidents give birth to
once you have learned how to let accidents happen
purposefully enough to beget ghosts.

Bird song is itself an accident,
a code no different from wolf howl, warthog grunt,
porpoise twitter. It is a way of placing
the cardinal in its sconce, of calling its hen,
of warning off others. *That* code. We hear it
and *re*-code it: it sounds to us like something
we might like to try. Who cares how it sounds
to another bird? We take what we need from nature,
not what is there. We can only guess what is there.

Guess then: why does no white bird sing
to our pleasure? Because, I will guess, songsters
nest in green-dapple. There, what is white shines.
What shines is visible. What is most visible
is soonest hunted. What is soonest hunted
becomes extinct. To sing, one must hide in the world
one sings from, colored to its accidents
which are never entirely accidents. Not when one sings.

The Lung Fish

For SPOOF, The Society for the Preservation of Old Fish, School of
Fisheries, University of Washington

In Africa, when river beds
    crack, the lung fish
squirms into mud deeper than
    the two feet down of wrath, and

sleeps, its tail over its eyes
    to keep them from drying blind, its
snout at a blow-hole blueprinted
    in the egg, too small to read,

but read. No one, the lung fish least,
    knows how long it can wait. If no
creature is immortal, some
    are more stubborn than others.

If all sleep is a miracle, consider
    (through the poking lenses
of unraveling science) what
    miracle this is: The lung fish

digests its own tissues. Its wastes,
    which are normally an ammonia
safely dispersed in water, would,
    in its cocoon, choke it. Therefore

it changes them to urea, which
    it can live with. Lung fish blood
is known to have six different
    hemoglobins—four more

than Moses took to God's desert.
    Like Moses, it has gone to legend
in Africa. It is said to be
    half fish, half croc. It is called

Kamongo there (but does not answer).
    If you cut off its head

(whether in fact or legend, and who
    knows which?) its jaws will snap

two days later. (Which
    we do know, all of us, about
what we cut off.) When
    Dr. Brown, an icthyologist

of Seattle, put Kamongo
    into a mud bottom aquarium
and lowered the water level, as God
    does at whim, this egg-born

instinctus of survival slept
    seventeen months. When it woke
in the reconfluence of time
    and whim, it seized stones with its mouth

and dinged them against the world's walls
    till it was fed—dinged them so hard
the doctor thought the walls might break
    between him and his creature. He drained it

back to sleep for time to build a world
    strong enough to hold both sleep
and waking. If anything can be. If we
    can learn sleep whole and not choke

on what we are while we learn it.

An Apartment with a View

I am in Rome, Vatican bells tolling
a windowful of God and Bernini.
My neighbor, the Pope, has died
and God overnight, has wept
black mantles over the sainted
stone age whose skirted shadows
flit through to the main cave.

I nurse a cold. It must be error
to sniffle in sight of holiness.
"Liquids," the doctor said. He has
no cure, but since I have my choice,
I sip champagne. If I must sit
dropsical to Heaven, let me at least
be ritual to a living water.

In the crypt under the cave
the stone box in its stone row
has been marked for months now.
My neighbor knew where he was going.
I half suspect I, too, know,
and that it is nothing to sneeze at,
but am left to sneeze.

I drink my ritual Moët et Chandon
and wish (my taste being misformed
for the high authentic) I had
a California—a Korbel
or an Almaden. I like it "forward,"
as clerics of such matters say,
not schooled to greatness.

It is loud in Heaven today
and in the great stone school
my neighbor kept.
The alumni procession of saints
is forming for him. Bells
clobber the air with portents.
I sniffle and sneeze,

wad kleenex, and sip champagne,
trying to imagine what it might be
to take part in a greatness,
or even in the illusion
of something-like. The experience
might deepen my character,
though I am already near

the bottom of it, among wads and butts
of what was once idea. And the last swallow.
I do not like the after-taste, if that
is what I am tasting. But this is ritual.
I toast my neighbor: may he
find his glass, and may its after-taste
be all that he was schooled to.

Jackstraws

The act of poetry, I submit, has been,
above all, prayer. Any anthology of it
is a jackstraw cathedral. Here and there
it sprouts its gargoyles. An erotica
of monkeys winks from Corinthian palm-tops.
Colin chucks Drusilla's country bubbles
in the shadows of the vestibule.—Cathedrals
can only aspire to Heaven: at groundlevel
they have to let everything in. And the poets
come to pray. Or, really, to have their prayers
overheard and, they hope, admired. Now then, if you
were the steeple-focused Thunderer, Pronouncer
of All Weathers, what would you make of prayers
delivered to an audience, and not for it,
but through it, for oneself? We are not simple.
Having invented God, we must confuse Him,
not because we want to but because
we are ourselves confused. Given this one
available universe as our *mis en scene,*
and no better audience than we ourselves make,
it could reasonably occur to us that prayer
might just be as confusingly out of context
as *The Tempest* staged in Death Valley. Ariel
dies dessicated. Caliban, being an ass,
can smell water. The scholar-duke, though reluctant,
must make an ass of himself, or die. It's not
what nature's child warbled his woodnotes to.
It's wilder. The duke is Norbert Wiener
programming a fourth-generation Ariel
Mark-10 Analogue compatible with
a Caliban retrieval system. And here come
building blocks. Though when you're tired giddy
of processing one more God from data's sand-blast,
it is fun (or at least it should be) to change channels
and to be in the audience when the poets pray.

Tuesday: Four Hundred Miles

Yesterday at the motel desk in Ocala
I could not remember my zip. Today
I can speak Etruscan. It came back.

It won't be called. It comes. And sometimes
my oath to Caesar, which need not be binding
in Ocala, but break it on the causeway

past Marathon Key and the sea is impassable:
you will be taken back, nailed upside down
to the cross, and be made to remember

sacred Marcia who stole from her parents
to run from honor with you. She died
of bad air from the marshes, but first knew

all the words to all the songs
she took with her. I can't even remember
the tunes, till they start uncalled.

It comes and goes and I stay wary.
I have grown a beard but keep moving
and avoid most public places. Old comrades

can see through hair, and it is death
to be recognized. I did not call
my life to these evasions, nor Marcia

to that fevered bed. It came.
Between Ostia and the Keys. In the new car
whose license number I can never remember.

Roman Diary: 1951

A rag woman, half a child,
with a soiled baby, half a bundle of rags,
whined on the Spanish Steps. It takes no words.

I reached into a pocket and found something.
She found words and a tune for them.
Even the flies on the baby rose to drone

Fransiscan *deo gratia.* "Hey!" said Coates,
"that was five hundred lira!" Coates had been there
over a month, was an old Roman hand

into everything but his own pocket.
"Don't you know they *rent* the babies?" he said.
"Everything in this crazy town is a racket!"

"We just ate didn't we?" I said—
he might have forgotten: the check
had slipped his mind—"let them eat."

"Ten suckers an hour like you and she'll take home
sixty-seventy bucks American.
That's damned well more than I can spend in a day!"

He was indignant! Why would he travel that far
to walk that tight for fear
the beggars were getting rich? I started to say—

—It wasn't worth it. Not the eighty cents,
not the big boodle in the poverty racket,
not a fool's fear he'd lose what he didn't have.

"If I go broke," I said, "I'll rent a baby."

Firts

At forty, home from traveled intention,
I could no longer speak my mother's dialect.

I had been in Italy rinsing my vowels.
She had been in Medford, Massachusetts

thickening her tongue on English crusts.
She had become a patois. What tongue was I?

I understood what I heard her say.
Could say it over and remember—ah, yes—

a taste like cooked wine-lees mushed with snow,
our winter *dolce* once. And how many years

not thought of, not forgotten? A taste
that slipped my tongue. Would I still like it, I doubt?

*   *   *

At times anywhere someone will say,
"Ah, you're from Boston!" And in Boston,

sooner or later, "Where are you from?"
Who in a last dark ever will call from his loss

as Dante was called, known by his cradle sounds
that spoke him to a birth and sharing?

Something still sits my tongue: that long "a"
down from the Hill, that "r" where no "r" is

I still catch myself sounding, surprised to hear it.
If anything speaks in Hell, it will be, alas,

the English Departments in whose cubicles
of lettered glass I numbered twenty years.

*   *   *

James Baldwin in back-Switzerland where no black man
had ever been, and they thought he was the devil,

sat a mountain, trapped in a Harvard accent,
and listened for months to Billie Holiday records

learning back Mama's cadence, ashamed to have lost
its glazed mornings, their first light of himself;

learning what had to be learned over. Like going back
to find a chimney in a wildrose thicket.

*   *   *

I remember losing the rifle my uncle gave me,
a single shot .22 from lathes in Heaven

to my twelfth birthday. I damned a dozen friends
I *knew* had stolen it. Till, ten years later,

Uncle—tired of his own bad wine, and clear
California gallons selling for less than it cost

to make his silty, cleared out the rack of barrels
—and there was the rifle, rusted shut, behind them.

And I put it out on the curb with the trash, and my shame
for what I had done with his gift, once perfect.

"Have I Said It True?"

Imagine putting all that talent
and all that passion
into as fuddy a duddy
as Emily Dickinson!

I believe in disguises.
Most real comes masked unlikely.
Or ask yourself: who
has ever seen you?

Stations

On being scared by a rattler while making a roadside relief stop
out in God's country.

An organization of clear purposes
braided hard as an Indian quirt,
the rattler coils and rings, instant
to the instant it lives.

It does not strike. Does it sense
my trembling recoil? I am nothing
to it. Not its food nor road-runner.
It warns and lets be. There's that

much mercy, thank you. What else
is it braided to? Escapes,
I suppose. The means of grace
food is to hunters. Burnt sand.

Hell must be full of rattlers, though
in a moral geography that interests us,
not them. (I am back in the car now
and can philosophize, air-conditioned

and manly in steel, glass, leather.
Next time, I think, shifting
to moral instruction, wait
for a gas station.) Meanwhile

if only to belittle fear, I ask
what God might have intended
when we imagine Him imagining
His patterns braided to venom.

Had I believed earlier and enough
I should have come in faith
and fearless to these ledges,
my hand open to the whip to prove

nothing harms saints
where all is an illuminated Godwork

of clear purposes braided hard.
What could such fangs be then

but witness to the intensity of God
shimmering through His own heat waves?
The pious beast at my feet
would have bitten its tail to omen

unending unbegun, its ornaments lavished
for the passtime joy of the making,
the Weaver's mood forever changing
on the constancy of His thread.

And having come so saint-braced
with the code of final intentions,
I need not have startled, and not run
to fantasize now a deadeye hipshot

I cannot make, leaving it headless
to thrash a ripple that washes out
under a spooked horse I, a tenderfoot,
could not have ridden to begin with.

Yet am I moralized as firmly as any
bestiary schools the pious: we are the beast
that must go when it must, but in God's
country keep to the stations.

For Miller Williams

Though Miller lives in Arkansas,
and though his back is bent,
the bush of beard that hides his jaw
like the Old Testament

is all his crop (and all his face).
When Miller parts that beard
the words come out and fall in place.
Were Miller to be sheared

there'd be a bag of wool for all.
And still the barefaced words
would find the thicket of man's fall
and settle it like birds.

There is a place in Miller's head
above, behind his bush,
where some of everything gets said
and nothing needs to push.

For everything comes out as whole
as once to Abraham,
as he was offering his son's soul
to God, there came the ram.

His father was a preacher,
a hilltop Methodist.
Miller is his own creature
but he has his father's gist

of hammering at God and man
remindfully. I doubt
he has his father's faith more than
as diction, but the words come out,

and every father, could he hear,
would do well to sit still
and listen and let down a tear,
as would have been God's will,

when God's will seemed to be a law
between the grave and shack
where holy mule-drawn Arkansas
pushed the ram's thicket back

and built a school and sent a son
who learned what he must say
of what is seen and felt and done
down to the roots of hay,

down to the pine-dark edge of sight,
down to the underbreath
that sugars sorghum and turns white
the chicken-shit of death.

Donne ch'avete intellètto d'amore

(An elegy for the American School System)

Mary and I were having an emotion.
"Thank you for having this emotion with me,"
Mary said, "I needed a reinforcement
of my identity through an interaction.
Have you accomplished a viable realization?"

"I know it was a formative experience,"
I said to Mary, "and yet, as I critique it
at my own level, I still feel under-achieved."

Mary touched me thoughtfully—reassurance
through personal contact. "Yes," she said, "I see."

"Is that susceptible of remediation?"
I said to Mary. Mary looked at the clock.
"I have a class to teach in an hour," she said,
"Do you feel you can wait?"—"Of course," I said,
        "if I must.
But frustration is always negative. May I suggest
a release-therapy impromptu now,
and a more fully structured enactment later?"

"All right," said Mary. We had a quick emotion.
"Was that an acceptable quick emotion?" I said.
"I do not wish to seem non-supportive," said Mary,
"but since you ask, permit me to stress the point
that an optimal interpersonal encounter
should emphasize mutuality. —Where are my pants?"

"Shall I drive you to class," I said as she was dressing.
"A truly empathetic response," said Mary,
"and approval is to be strongly indicated
as tendency re-inforcement in trait-development.
But might it not be even more constructive
for you to sit here and to introspect
a clarification of your personal goals?"

"It will also give me a chance to shower," I said.

"Mens sana in corpore sano," she said at the door.
"I shall be looking forward to relating fully
To your raised consciousness." And she smiled and left.

O intellect of love, may I prove worthy!

A Crate of Sterling Loving Cups

I had gone to a freightyard auction of sealed crates.
Like parenthood, you bid, then see what you've got.
Mine opened to an idea: I was sure I knew
enough beautiful people to give them out to.

The engraving couldn't cost much: *This cup is presented*
to X-X-X from our shared transcience
in recognition of at least one moment
in which the donor thought YOU ARE BEAUTIFUL.

I had the first in mind for Archie MacLeish.
I'd have to come down a notch to find a second,
but the precedent would be set. To qualify
one would have, by God, to qualify. What are we

if we can't choose example? —A local fool
printed the story with application forms.
As if one could apply to be beautiful.
In a sense, I suppose, one must, but supporting letters,

especially from one's mother, do not count.
Nor fair employment practices. Nor guide-lines
from the grinning presidency. Nor minority pickets
blatting definition from a bullhorn.

I have nothing to say to this mindless generation
that thinks to be chosen rare by filling blanks
in my fool neighbor's forms. This mail is his.
I dump the daily basketful at his door

and burn what he returns to me. Soon now
I shall be leaving for Key West for the winter.
My house there is un-numbered, my phone unlisted.
It will do no good to try me as OCCUPANT:

you won't have found me till I answer, and I
shall be busy reading. The contest is called off.
(I'm sorry, Archie. New postal regulations
forbid the mailing of anything real and accurate.)

When I get back I shall have them melted down—
or hammered, or whatever it is one does—
into something useful. I'd like a large tureen
with a matching ladle. I do make a good soup.

What's left could make bowls enough and spoons enough
to set a table for a trial guest list.
Or even for a more-or-less open house.
Soup is a good that doesn't invite ambition.